PERCEIVING ENERGY

*To my children,
Clark, Katherine Elise and Christopher,
who freely embrace unlimited ways of "seeing"*

ACKNOWLEDGEMENTS

Infinite gratitude to Aarron Light for his ever present support and inspiration. My love and thanks to Flora and Dietmar Graf for their support and encouragement.

A multitude of thanks to a thoughtful benefactor, whose care for the environment and support for global awareness prompted an exceedingly generous contribution of paper used for the creation of this book and others I have written.

I would like to acknowledge each and every reader for having the courage to change the way they "see" the world around them.

HOW TO CONTACT THE AUTHOR

Dr. Dawn E. Clark presents lectures, seminars and workshops for individuals, businesses, associations and non-profit organizations nationwide. For information please visit the web site or write the address below. Readers of this book are also encouraged to write with comments or experiences.

Web Site: **Infinite-EnergyLinks.com**

Address: **Infinite EnergyLinks, Inc.**
P.O. Box 5485
Kingwood, TX 77325

ATTENTION ORGANIZATIONS, HEALING CENTERS AND SCHOOLS OF SPIRITUAL DEVELOPMENT:

Quantity discounts are available on bulk purchases of this book for educational purposes or fund raising. Special books or book excerpts can also be created to fit special needs. For information, please contact Aarron Publishing, P.O. Box 271203, Houston, TX 77277-1203 or e-mail Aarronpublishing@hotmail.com.

PERCEIVING ENERGY

Beyond the Physical Form

Dawn E. Clark, Ph.D.

AARRON
PUBLISHING

Perceiving Energy
Copyright © 1999 by Dawn E. Clark
Printed and bound in the United States of America

All rights reserved. No part of this book may be reproduced by any mechanical, photographic, or electronic process, or in the form of a recording, nor may it be stored in a retrieval system, transmitted, or otherwise be copied for public or private use without written permission from the publisher. For information, please address Aarron Publishing, P.O. Box 271203, Houston, TX 77277-1203.

Important Note for the Reader:
The author, editors, and publisher cannot be held responsible for the consequences of trying the ideas, suggestions, and techniques in this book. The ideas, suggestions, and techniques in this book should not be used in place of sound medical therapies and recommendations.

FIRST EDITION

Library of Congress Catalog Card Number: 99-90425
ISBN: 1-928532-02-0 (PBK)
99 00 01 02 03 v AP 10 9 8 7 6 5 4 3 2

This book is printed on acid-free paper.

Contents

1	**HOW TO USE THIS BOOK**	9
2	**TUNING IN TO YOUR HIGHER AWARENESS**	11
	Universal Energy	12
	Introductory Exercise for Increasing Intuitive Perception	13
3	**THE POWER OF VISUALIZATION**	17
	Activating Your Mind's-Eye	18
	Forming Mental Images	18
4	**WHAT IS AN ENERGY FIELD**	21
	Tactile Perception of an Inanimate Object's Energy Field	22

		Exercise in Tactile Perception	23
		COLOR IN ENERGY	27
		COLOR FREQUENCY CORRELATIONS	27
		Feeling and Intuiting Color	27
5	PERCEIVING THE ENERGY OF LIVING THINGS		31
		PERCEIVING ENGERY IN NATURE	34
		Feeling Energy in Nature	34
		Perceiving Energetic Color in Nature with the Mind's-Eye	40
6	ENERGETIC SYNCHRONICITY		43
		Synchronicity in Action	44
		Comparing Indoor and Outdoor Plants	45
7	THE HUMAN ENERGY FIELD		47
		CHAKRAS	49
		THE NINE MAJOR ENERGY CENTERS	51
		Developing Tactile Perception of the Human Energy Field or Aura	56
		Third-Eye Perception of Color in the Human Energy Field	61
		Changing the Field	65
8	EMPATHY		67
9	VISUAL PERCEPTION OF AURA		69
		Strengthening Optic Perception	69
		Visual Perception of Tree Auras	73
		VISUALLY PERCEIVING THE HUMAN ENERGY FIELD	76

Contents

Visually Perceiving Your Own Aura	76
Visually Perceiving Someone Else's Aura	79
VISUAL PERCEPTION OF COLOR IN THE AURA	81
COLOR DESCRIPTIONS	82
Developing Visual Color Perception of Your Own Aura	84
Seeing Color in Aura I	86
Seeing Color in Aura II	89
Seeing Color in Aura III	93
AURIC TIME ZONES	97
10 AUDITORY CLAIRVOYANCE	101
Hearing Energetic Vibrations I	102
Hearing Energetic Vibrations II	104
Hearing Energetic Vibrations III	107
11 PSYCHOMETRY	111
Practicing Psychometry	111
12 THE ENERGY OF PLACES	115
13 PERCEIVING GUIDES	117
How to Perceive Angels or Guides	117
14 SENSE THE DIFFERENCE	121
RESOURCES	123

1
HOW TO USE THIS BOOK

This book is designed to be a practical, straightforward guide for expanding your inter-dimensional perception. *You can perceive energy.*

As early as age three, I can remember seeing clouds of auric color surrounding people. Over the years it has brought me great joy to help others unlock their own natural abilities to perceive.

Are you ready to join the small handful of people who can see and feel dynamic energy fields? Everyone can do it. Each of us possesses the natural gifts of heightened sensory perception, telepathic communication and intuitive guidance. These are not special talents given only to a select few, but are inherent within us all. We are naturally clairvoyant, yet our abilities to perceive energy often lie latent within us.

In everyday life, you have probably already noticed that one or two of your senses are inherently stronger and more dominant. For example, a heightened sense of touch may cause you to experience increased sensitivity to tactile stimulation, such as the texture of fabrics against your skin. A strong sense smell or taste may foster exceptional pleasure in culinary delights or cause great sensitivity to odors. Being visually adept may enable you to see at great distances, have excellent night vision, or allow you to easily discern minute shades of color variation. And, a keen sense of hearing may cause you to be noise sensitive, yet be able to hear conversations in the next room. What are your strengths or dominant senses in third dimensional perception? What are your recessive or less dominant senses?

You will have natural strengths in perceiving energy as well. This book is designed to enhance these strengths and offer a variety of techniques by which to experience dynamic energy fields. Some methods will come more naturally and quickly than others. Overtime, with practice, you can learn to do them all.

Within this book you will find easy-to-follow techniques to reawaken your hidden gifts of heightened sensory perception. Each exercise builds one upon the other and should be done in progression to maximize your inner potential. Take your time and enjoy the process.

You, too, can perceive energy!

2
TUNING IN TO YOUR HIGHER AWARENESS

There are many ways to perceive energy. You can perceive through sight, sound, smell, taste, touch, intuition and visualization. A good place to begin reawakening your perceptual abilities is by tuning into your inner knowing or "higher self."

Listening to your inner voice and intuitive guidance, as opposed to following the norms or ideas dictated by society, is often necessary to achieve heightened energetic perception. This can be difficult for the ego because it involves facing the unknown and admitting that things exist which your physical eyes cannot yet see.

When you begin these exercises, your ego may react with, "If it was real, you could see it!" Through statements such as these, which we may be only barely conscious of, the ego convinces us not to move ahead by insisting, "It's all nonsense. You are fooling yourself." In this way the ego causes us to doubt what our extra sensory perceptions are discerning.

This is when inner knowing and the ability to connect with universal energy become indispensable. Remain in faith. Remember that the ego is fear driven and does not like change or growth. Follow your heart; expand your horizons.

Intuitive guidance is available to us all through inner knowing, visualization, meditation and dream. Anyone who chooses to can learn to heighten their sensory perceptions and access the intuitive guidance available through the continuum of universal energy.

Universal Energy

Where do knowings like, "I knew it was him calling," or "I had a feeling that was going to happen," come from? The knowing you are experiencing is based on information transmitted through the Universal Energy Field. If someone is projecting a thought or idea, you can easily tune in to this energy projection. The first step is to quiet your mind enough to hear the knowing.

Universal energy connects all things. It surrounds us, interpenetrates us, and makes an energetic continuum available for the reception of information, telepathic communication and manifestation. The concept of a Universal Energy Field has existed for millennia and permeates many cultures. Differing cultures have called this energy by various names. In India, for example, universal energy has been known as *prana* for over 5,000 years. This force, *prana*, is believed to permeate all life. Similarly, over 4,000 years ago, the Chinese gave the name of *chi* to the universal energy believed to surround and compose all matter; *chi* is believed to be the source of all life.

To access the information available within the Universal Energy Field, we must tune in to our inner knowing. This is a form of energetic perception in and of itself.

Introductory Exercise for Increasing Intuitive Perception

One of the easiest ways to awaken your inner voice, so that you can begin to "hear," is to play a game with yourself by asking your intuition to answer questions like those in the following exercise.

Please note that when people become aware of their inner voice, or intuition, most do not actually hear a "voice" speaking to them in their ear or in their head. Information is generally received as a flash of knowing or an idea.

Quiet your mind and pay attention to your first impulses. They are usually correct. The later or secondary "voice" tends to be the ego arguing with the intuition.

Sample practice questions for tuning in to your intuition:

1. Who is calling on the telephone?

2. Has the mail come yet?

3. Which team will win?

4. Do I have e-mail? If so, how many?

5. Which checkout line at the grocery store will move quicker?

6. Will the stock market index rise or fall?

Feel free to create your own questions.

The new intuitive capability you are developing is like a muscle that has not been used in a long while. Time and practice are required to build your strength and confidence. Positive reinforcement is important.

When your inner voice proves to be right, pat yourself on the back and take notice. This acknowledgment helps you become ever more aware of your inner knowing. Keep track of your successes for two weeks and you will be pleasantly surprised to see how quickly your accuracy increases.

Intuition manifests in many ways ranging from quiet knowings to strong gut feelings. You may even experience flashes of visuals before your eyes. Being able to tune in to your inner knowing is key to many types of energetic perception. Continue to practice heightening your awareness as you proceed with the subsequent exercises.[1]

---

[1] For more information on accessing intuitive guidance, please reference the author's work entitled *Tuning In: Opening Your Intuitive Channels*.

3
THE POWER OF VISUALIZATION

In addition to being aware of your inner knowing, the ability to visualize can be key for beginning energy perception, particularly until the physical eyes are trained and the optic nerves developed. Unfortunately, in our television-computer-laden era, we are bombarded with such a plethora of external visual stimuli that our ability to visualize has been largely lost. Many children today are so overwhelmed by external visual imagery that they have difficulty listening to a book being read aloud and "watching" the pictures unfold in their mind's-eye or imagination. They, too, have lost their ability to visualize.

Visualization is a powerful tool for translating your heightened sensory perceptions into visual images. Reactivating your ability to visualize simply requires quieting your mind and some practice. Let's begin by learning a simple technique for activating your mind's-eye.

Activating Your Mind's-Eye

1. Find a comfortable position and relax.

2. Close your eyes. Breathe slowly and effortlessly.

3. With your eyes closed, shift your eyes slightly upward and tilt your head slightly backward.

This precursor exercise to visualization assists in activating the third-eye or mind's-eye. It also accesses visual images and opens a channel for visual interpretations from a variety of sensory perceptions.

Forming Mental Images

Now that your inner eye has been activated, let us practice visualizing. Please read through the entire exercise before beginning, and remember that imagination is a key component in visualization.

1. Find a comfortable position. Close your eyes

and take a few deep, cleansing breaths.

2. Imagine a large, yellow lemon with a perfect, blemish free peel. This lemon is the perfect color, the perfect temperature and the perfect ripeness.

3. With your eyes closed, slowly let the feeling of the picture come to you.

4. Stay with the feeling and a picture will begin to form. You may just barely be able to see it. Be patient, don't try to push or speed up the process. The picture may come from any direction and can actually form itself off to the side rather than in front.

5. Begin to employ your senses of smell, touch, taste, and hearing until the picture becomes clear. How does the lemon smell? How does its skin feel against your fingertips?

6. Next, imagine cutting the lemon in half. Listen to the sound of the knife as it slices through the fruit.

7. Next, visualize picking up half of the lemon and squeezing the lemon's juice into your mouth. How does it taste? Is your mouth watering?

Repeat the exercise with other objects or ideas, such as a juicy, ripe peach or a perfect vacation spot. Continue to practice until you are able to visualize with ease. This skill, coupled with tuning in to your higher awareness, will be a powerful asset as you continue to develop your perception of energy fields.

4
WHAT IS AN ENERGY FIELD ?

We live in a fluid world of energy that is constantly in motion. Nothing is really solid or concrete. Science has shown that matter is simply slowed down or crystallized energy. Even our physical bodies are made up of energy.

Everything is connected through and permeated by universal energy. The interaction between this energy, or life force, and physical structures produces additional perceivable effects, such as auric projection, sound and vibration. Understanding this concept can be most helpful as you begin to perceive the energy fields that surround you.

Cleve Backster, a pioneer in the field of auric documentation caused a great stir in 1968, when he announced that plants have emotions, memory and

ESP. Backster, a recognized polygraph expert and owner of the Backster School of Lie Detection of New York, utilized polygraph analysis to reach the following conclusions:

- ❃ Plants record a measurable reaction on a lie detector when any living thing dies in their presence.

- ❃ Plants seem to recognize owners and respond to the thoughts and emotions of those around them.

- ❃ Plants have aura as evidenced by the missing leaf phenomenon, which is similar to the missing limb phenomenon experienced by amputees.

All things project an energetic signature or vibration. When you are able to perceive energy and the array of colors and sounds associated with the vibrations, your surroundings take on an entirely new perspective.

Tactile Perception of an Inanimate Object's Energy Field

Kinesthetic or tactile perception of energy fields is possible for everyone. One of the quickest ways to develop this ability is to begin by practicing with inanimate objects such as large rocks or crystals.

The following exercise will employ your sense of touch, intuition and visualization, rather than your physical eyes. Initially utilizing this approach is beneficial because society has conditioned us to believe that "what we can't see, doesn't exist." This, of course, is a fallacy.

It is not necessary to be able to see with your eyes. Feeling is equally valid, as are other methods of perception. Energetic vibrations for example, are easily perceptible through a kinesthetic medium. Many people never choose to develop their visual perception of energy. Instead, they rely on their abilities to intuit, hear, feel, visualize, taste and smell energy.

Exercise in Tactile Perception

For the following exercise you will need a large rock or crystal and a pencil for sketching your mind's-eye interpretation of what you feel. Please read the entire exercise before beginning.

1. Place a large rock or crystal on a cleared table.

2. Stand with the stone or crystal positioned on the table in front of you.

3. Close your eyes and position your left hand palm down, high over the object. By not employing your visual perception at this time,

you will be better able to focus on the perceptions of your left hand, which is the natural hand for energetic reception and therefore more readily sensitive.

4. Very slowly allow your hand to descend over the object.

5. Become aware of the increased energetic density as you near the object. This density may be perceived as a thickening of the air, or it may have a quality of temperature, prickles, pulsations or waves.

    Also, if you are working with a crystal the energy field may present like a shaft with linear qualities, whereas a stone's energy will tend to be more rounded. Remember energetic vibrations are perceptible in a variety of ways.

6. As you discern the edge of the energy field, stop and open your eyes. Look at how far above the object you are.

7. Sketch the stone or crystal along with your perception of its energy field in the following space provided.

8. Continue scanning the object from different directions. Do this several times and sketch the results. Are all sides of the rock's or crystal's energy field equal in density and height? Or does one side extend further than another?

PERCEIVING ENERGY

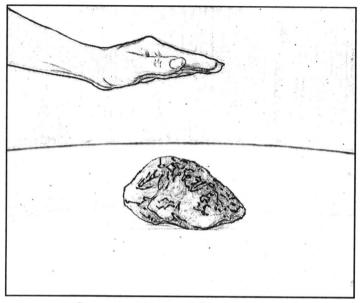

Scanning Energy of Quartz Crystal

Initially, as you scan the rock or stone, you may perceive the density of the energy field only a few inches from the object itself. As you become more sensitive to higher vibrating energies, you will be able to detect energetic fields further from the object. Be sure to experiment with both stones and crystals.

Draw your own perceptions here:

Color in Energy

As you scan energy fields, your higher self knows what your hand is perceiving and is even able to recognize the energetic frequencies of varying colors. Support of energetic colors having identifiable frequencies can be found in a 1988 study done at UCLA by Dr. Valorie Hunt, which demonstrated that auric color perceptions by clairvoyants could be correlated with specific hertz frequency ranges. The following are basic color/frequency correlations based on her study.

Color Frequency Correlations

Blue	250-275 Hz plus 1200 Hz
Green	250-475 Hz
Yellow	500-700 Hz
Orange	950-1050 Hz
Red	1000-1200 Hz
Violet	1000-2000 Hz, plus 300-400; 600-800 Hz
White	1100-2000 Hz

Feeling and Intuiting Color

We will now broaden the previous exercise by combining your tactile perception of energy with intuition and visualization in order to perceive color as well as density. You will need a box of crayons and a large stone or crystal.

1. Place a large stone or crystal on a cleared table.

2. Stand with the stone or crystal positioned on the table in front of you.

3. Close your eyes and position your left hand palm down, high over the object.

4. Keeping your eyes closed, allow yourself to become aware of what you are sensing with your left hand.

5. Very slowly lower your hand over the object.

6. Once your hand senses the energy field of the crystal or stone, allow your hand to remain in the field.

7. After a few seconds, silently ask what color you are feeling. The answer will usually just pop into your head, or you may get a visual image of a specific color in your mind's-eye.

8. Trust the information you receive. Listen to your intuition. Based on my experience teaching classes in energetic perception, beginning students intuit correctly approximately eighty percent of the time when they listen to their first impressions.

9. Sketch the object and color it's energy field with the colors you perceived in the following space provided.

PERCEIVING ENERGY

10. Continue to scan and perceive auric colors from various sides of the object. It is important to note that an object can have more than one color.

11. Record you findings. Did you perceive more than one color? Was the energy field equal on all sides?

This exercise stimulates your third-eye's capabilities and is a precursor to visual perception of energy. Repeat this procedure with different types of stones and crystals. The more you practice, the greater your skill level will become.

5
PERCEIVING THE ENERGY OF LIVING THINGS

The energy fields, or aura, which radiate from a life form are related to the universal energy that interpenetrates the physical body. As such, aura emits characteristics distinctive to the life form itself. As you begin perceiving the energy of living things, understanding the four basic levels of aura is highly beneficial. These levels or layers can be experienced in plants, animals and humans.

- ❋ The first is the physical level, which is the densest and lies closest to the body.

- ❋ The second is the emotional level. This auric layer is the easiest to come in contact with, lies next to the physical level, and is often felt and seen in waves or pulses. This layer can also be perceived as flowing, spinning, or creating flashes.

When scanning through this layer, you may experience some of the other person's current emotions or receive visual flashes of information via your mind's-eye.

The emotional level is readily connected with the heart chakra and can transmit energy to another person over great distances. It is also through this level that a bad mood can be projected from one person to another.

* The mental level is the third layer. At this level ideas and thought forms can be perceived projecting from a person.

* The fourth layer, and the most difficult to tune in to because of its high vibration, is the inspirational or spiritual level.

Auric layers interpenetrate and surround each other. Each successive layer is composed of higher vibrating energy than the layer it surrounds. When you initially begin to perceive energy, the physical and emotional layers are the easiest to sense because they are the densest.

Perceiving Energy

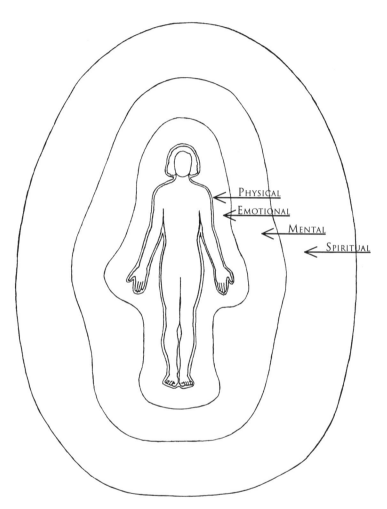

Four Basic Layers of Aura

Perceiving Energy in Nature

We will now begin a series of exercises designed to heighten your perception of energies in nature. It has been my experience that people are able to feel the energy of trees more readily than they can sometimes perceive their own energy bodies. A number of factors account for this. However, one of the leading causes is existing energetic shutdown and blockage in the perceiver's aura.

Feeling Energy in Nature

Read the entire exercise before beginning. You will need a pencil for sketching.

1. Go outside or to a park where there are many large, healthy trees.

2. Look around. One tree will draw your attention.

3. Go over to the tree and silently thank it for helping you learn and grow.

4. Kneel down slightly to the left of the tree.

5. Extend your left hand, at a height of approximately six inches above the ground, as far out from the left side of the tree trunk as you can.

Perceiving Energy

6. Close your eyes and take a deep, cleansing breath.

7. Now, with your left hand still in position six inches above the ground, slowly bring your hand in toward the tree trunk.

8. Tune in to your hand's tactile perception. As you move closer to the trunk, the energy will become denser. When you begin to feel a change or shift in density, open your eyes and look at how far from the tree trunk your hand is positioned. This shift in density is the boundary of one of the tree's auric layers.

9. Close your eyes again and continue scanning toward the tree trunk. As you move closer, the energy's density will continue to increase. At some point, you will feel as though you have reached another energetic wall or boundary. For beginners this usually occurs in the last inch before you reach the trunk.

10. When you have found the boundary of the auric layer, open your eyes again and check your hand position.

11. Sketch the energy fields you felt in the space provided at the end of this exercise. As your sensitivity to higher vibrations increases, you will be able to perceive a tree's aura from greater distances.

12. Once you have been able to scan the energy at the base of the tree, stand up and scan the tree again about five feet higher up the trunk. (Refer to steps 8-10)

13. Once again, sketch the energy you perceived in the following space provided.

14. Assess your perceptions. Did the energy feel different at a height of five feet above the ground than it did at the base of the tree? Was it less or more dense? Did it seem to be flowing as if it were a stream? Or did it float like a cloud? Or pulsate?

Scanning Base of Tree

PERCEIVING ENERGY

Sketch your perceptions:

Continue your practice with shrubs and other healthy outdoor plants until you are confident in your newfound abilities. Please refrain from practicing with indoor plants until you have read the section on energetic synchronicity.

Scanning Outdoor Plants

Sketch your perceptions of outdoor plants:

Take your time. Don't try to become an expert in one day. We all have the inherent ability to perceive energy. However, as with most new skills, time is required to fully develop them.

Perceiving Energetic Color in Nature with the Mind's-Eye

This exercise combines your visualization skills, your ability to feel energy fields and your intuitive perception of energetic color.

Once again, please find a tree to work with. You will also need crayons or colored pencils.

1. Go outside or to a park where there are many large, healthy trees.

2. Look around. One tree will seem to draw your attention.

3. Walk over to the tree and silently thank it for helping you learn and grow.

4. Kneel down slightly to the left of the tree.

5. Extend your left hand, at a height of approximately six inches above the ground, as far out from the side of the tree trunk as you can.

6. Close your eyes and take a deep, cleansing breath.

7. Now, with your left hand still in position six inches above the ground, begin to scan inward toward the tree trunk. Tune in to your hand's tactile perception.

8. Once you feel the tree's aura, stop and allow your hand to remain in the field. Silently ask what color the energy you are perceiving is. The answer will usually just pop into your head, or you may get a visual image of a specific color in your mind's-eye.

9. Sketch and color your perceptions.

10. Continue by scanning the tree at different heights, stopping to perceive auric colors with your mind's-eye.

11. Record your findings.

12. Assess your results. How many auric layers did you sense? What colors did you perceive? Did the energy pulsate or flow? Did any sections feel as if the energy was rushing by, or did it feel more like a motionless cloud?

Sketch and color your perceptions on the following page.

Continue to practice with shrubs and other outdoor plants. Give yourself time to build strength in your newfound skills. Please read the next section on energetic synchronicity before scanning indoor plants.

6
ENERGETIC SYNCHRONICITY

Synchronicity of energy fields is a common side effect of cohabitation. This phenomenon can be seen in household pets. Over the course of time, indoor pets often take on the auric colors of their owners in an effort to blend in and match their primary caretaker's vibration. This mirroring procedure tends to take two to five years and helps explain why owners of older pets sometimes feel that their pets have become almost "human." Energetic synchronicity occurs in household plants as well, but requires a far shorter period of time.

Synchronicity in Action

An experiment to demonstrate this phenomenon can be done with indoor household plants. This experiment requires the participation of a friend and one new household plant.

1. Without you being present, have a friend place a new plant in their house among other plants that have been there for some time. You are not to know which is the new plant upon entry into the room. It is best to perform this experiment the first day the new plant is in the house.

2. Once you enter the room, scan each plant tactilely, visually and intuitively with a closed-eye color visualization to see if you can detect a perceptible difference between them.

3. The new plant should be easy to spot. Its energy will be distinctly different from the other plants whose energies have synchronized into a more homogenous hum. The new plant's energetic vibration will not yet match the energies of the other household plants.

Follow Up:

Have your friend keep the plant in close proximity to the other plants for at least two weeks. Then, follow-up with the experiment below.

1. This time, have your friend blindfold you and place the plants in front of you.

2. Tactilely scan and visualize the energy fields. What did you find? Were you able to detect a significant difference between the plants?

If the plants have been kept in close proximity to each other, there should be little discernible difference. The new plant will be nearing vibrational synchronicity with the other houseplants.

Comparing Indoor and Outdoor Plants

For this exercise you will need an indoor and outdoor plant of approximately the same size.

1. Scan and intuitively perceive the colors of both the indoor and outdoor plant's energy fields.

2. Sketch your findings below.

3. How did the fields differ? Did the outdoor plant or the indoor plant have the larger field? How did the color and flow of the fields compare?

Realizing the energetic implications of cohabitation will deepen your understanding of energy fields and help refine your perceptions.

7
THE HUMAN ENERGY FIELD

Many people today, as products of the Scientific Age, are reluctant to accept the presence of a Human Energy Field or aura until it is "proven" to them. Unfortunately, until we have experienced it, until we have learned to see it or feel it, we tend to dismiss its very existence. In doing so, we deny ourselves a tremendous healing resource.

Historical support for the Human Energy Field abounds.

- ❖ Hindu Vedic texts, Native American beliefs and Buddhism all have elaborate descriptions of the Human Energy Field.

- ❈ The Kabbalah, the book of ancient Jewish mysticism, refers to universal and human energy as "astral light."

- ❈ The Pythagoreans in 500 B.C. wrote of seeing a "luminous body" or energy surrounding the physical body.

- ❈ The Bible has numerous references to a luminescence, or light, surrounding people.

- ❈ NBC aired results of studies showing the ability of auric energy to bend or affect the beam projected by a small two-milliwatt laser.

The Human Energy Field or aura is related to the universal energy field's interpenetration of our physical body, as well as the energy we radiate from our feelings, thoughts and physical being. It can be perceived through its unique vibration and density and can be seen as a bubble of light or color surrounding the body.

The aura has a direct correlation to a person's emotional, psychological and physiological states. All of your outer and inner expressions result in a manifestation of light vibration. Past emotional traumas or abuse often cause "shutdowns" or a cessation of energy flow through certain regions of the body. If these shutdowns are allowed to remain for long periods of time, a physical manifestation of illness usually occurs within the body.

The interrelation between the physical body and

the metaphysical energy body is one reason why black or gray colors in the aura can be reflective of diseased physical tissue.

CHAKRAS

By realizing that *chi* or universal energy flows through our physical bodies, a better understanding of chakras can be achieved. Chakras are energy centers through which universal energy flows and nurtures us, all the while making available a plethora of information. We in turn project our own unique energetic signature. This constant flow of energy can be likened to sea water flowing in and out of a sponge.

The name chakra is derived from an East Indian word for wheel, and in fact, when these energy centers are open and activated, the energy associated with them does spin like a wheel. Furthermore, when open and activated each chakra projects a flow of vibrating energy through it that creates a color and sound corresponding to its location in the body.

When an energy center or energy flow through the physical body is blocked, the light, or energy, which is normally able to pass through it, will be slowed and appear gray or dull reflecting the change in energetic vibration. Supporting evidence is found in Dr. Dora Kunz' study, which documented that diseased tissue, or tissue which had been affected by surgery, had mismatched energetic rhythms when compared to healthy tissue.

Each chakra reflects the energetic health of a particular aspect of our mental-emotional expression. In addition, the amount of energy flowing through each chakra affects specific aspects of our physical bodies. Blockages of energy through the body's chakras and energy meridians diminish our mental, emotional and physical well-being. By re-establishing energy flow, energetic meridians are activated, thereby enabling us to access information contained in physical cell tissue, old memories and etheric information.[2]

---

[2] For more information and images that instantly open chakras and energy meridians, please see the author's work entitled *Gifts for the Soul*.

PERCEIVING ENERGY

The Nine Major Energy Centers

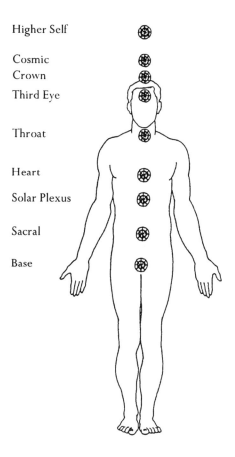

Higher Self

Cosmic
Crown

Third Eye

Throat

Heart

Solar Plexus

Sacral

Base

1. **The Base or Power Chakra** is located at the base of the spine and when open, emanates the color red. This chakra represents sex as well as survival and pertains to how assertively we seek our goals. Open base chakras dramatically increase capabilities for manifesting.

2. **The Sacral Chakra** lies in the abdominal area just below the navel. It is related to the reproductive system and emanates the color orange when open. This energy center is reflective of a body's vitality and health and relates to overall connection of energy meridians.

3. **The Solar Plexus or Creative Chakra** lies in the upper stomach region or solar plexus, which is located at the soft tissue just under the breastbone. This center is where our "gut" feelings originate and it vibrates the color yellow. Our thoughts, ideas and willpower are reflected in this chakra, and much of our intuitive guidance about other people comes from energetic connections originating in this center.

4. **The Heart Chakra** lies in the middle of the sternum approximately two fingers' width above the bottom of the breastbone. This center is utilized to feel and understand others so that we may live in harmony and balance. This chakra emanates a beautiful grass green that can often be seen streaming forth in magnificent radiance from those who are newly in love. Negative emotions such as vanity, jealousy, guilt, regret and envy can cause the heart chakra to shut down.

5. **The Throat Chakra** is located in the hollow area just below the Adam's Apple and vibrates sky blue. This center's primary purpose is communication.

6. **The Third-Eye Chakra** is located on the forehead in between the eyes and is responsible for visualization and pictures in dreams or meditation. When open, this chakra vibrates indigo and can become a powerful tool for telepathy.

7. **The Crown Chakra** lies at the top of head and usually emanates clear or white. Often as one progresses along a healing journey, the crown will begin to open, and the energy sensations associated with the newfound energy flow can feel like tingling or itchy scalp.

8. **The Cosmic Chakra** lies approximately six inches above the crown, represents our link to universal thought and is silver in color. Deeper understanding of basic universal principles, such as karma, abundance, the oneness of everything and reincarnation, is facilitated through this chakra.

9. **The Higher Self Chakra**, located approximately eighteen inches above the crown chakra, is the center of higher enlightenment and provides a great sense of inner peace and knowing. When open, this energy center vibrates gold and provides protection by enabling the transmutation of negative energy.

Having blockages, or even complete shutdowns, in your energy field is common as you begin your healing journey. Many illnesses are in actuality the physical manifestations of energy shutdowns in the Human Energy Field. As energy ceases to flow to certain areas, disease is allowed into the body through the subconscious suppression of the immune system, negative self-programming and the accumulation of toxins.

The following chart shows the basic correlation between the physical body's seven major chakras and their physiological counterparts.

Chakra	Associated Endocrine Gland	Related Area of Body
Crown	Pineal	Upper Brain; Right Eye
Third-Eye	Pituitary	Lower Brain; Left Eye; Ears; Nose; Nervous System; associated with Seeing
Throat	Thyroid	Lungs; Vocal Apparatus; Alimentary Canal; Hearing; Smelling; Tasting
Heart	Thymus	Heart; Blood; Vagus Nerve; Circulatory System
Solar Plexus	Pancreas	Stomach; Liver; Gallbladder; Nervous System; Spleen
Sacral	Gonads	Reproductive System; Hypogastric
Base	Adrenals	Spinal Column; Kidneys; associated with Touch

It is also interesting to note that the seven major chakras associated with the physical body have frontal and rear aspects in relation to the body. The frontal is the emotional aspect of the chakra and the rear tends to relate to the aspect of will in each energy center.

Developing Tactile Perception of the Human Energy Field or Aura

This exercise requires a partner and a pencil for sketching your findings. Please note that when you begin perceiving other people's auras, it is imperative that you have their permission. Violation of another's space and energy without consent is not ethical.

1. Begin by standing to the side and slightly in front of your partner, so that your left hand can enter the energy field in front of your partner's heart chakra.

2. Begin with your left hand approximately three feet away from your partner's body.

3. Close your eyes and take a deep cleansing breath. By keeping your eyes closed during this exercise, perceptions through your tactile senses and your higher awareness are encouraged, as opposed to trying to "see" with your physical eyes at this time.

4. Move your hand very slowly towards the heart chakra.

PERCEIVING ENERGY

Scanning the Human Energy Field

5. Stop when you feel a change in energetic density. You are at an auric layer. These layers are often perceived as a shift in density, temperature or sensation. Remember everybody perceives or takes in information differently. All perceptions are valid.

6. Open your eyes and note how far from the body your are.

7. Close your eyes again and continue to scan toward the body. When you feel shifts in energetic density, heat or sensation, stop.

8. At each layer you sense, open your eyes and see how much closer you are to your partner's physical body. A novice scanner will usually be able to perceive one or two auric layers with a little practice.

9. Continue the exercise by scanning your partner's energy field from a variety of sides until you have a good idea of the aura's size.

10. Sketch what you perceived on the diagrams provided. Is the aura equally distributed?

PERCEIVING ENERGY

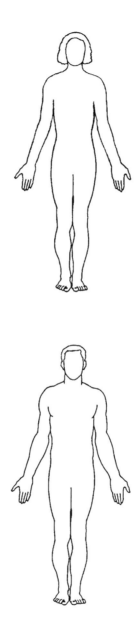

Try repeating the exercise with a partner of the opposite sex and see if you notice any differences. Practice this exercise until you feel proficient at perceiving at least two auric levels.

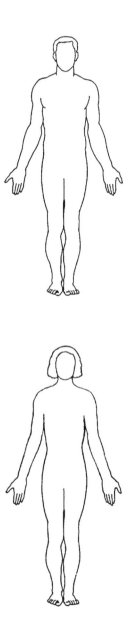

Third-Eye Perception of Color in the Human Energy Field

If possible, continue working with a partner you previously practiced with. You will need a box of crayons or colored pencils.

1. Begin by standing to the side and slightly in front of your partner, so that your left hand can enter the energy field in front of your partner's heart chakra.

2. Position your left hand at arm's length, approximately three feet in front of your partner's heart chakra.

3. Close your eyes and take a deep cleansing breath. Closing your eyes during this exercise encourages perception with your tactile senses, your higher awareness, and your mind's-eye.

4. Move your hand very slowly towards the body.

5. Stop when you feel a change in energetic density. You are at an auric layer. These layers are often perceived as a shift in density, temperature or sensation. Remember everybody perceives or takes in information differently. All perceptions are valid.

6. With your eyes still closed, allow your hand to remain in the energy field. Silently ask what color you are sensing. The answer will usually just pop into your head as a knowing, or you may perceive a visual image of the color in your mind's-eye.

7. Once you have received the answer, record your findings on the diagrams which follow.

8. Continue to scan from a variety of sides and heights. Stop and intuitively assess the color each time.

9. Record your findings on the next page.

10. Assess your findings. How many colors did you find? Did you feel waves or swirls in the energy? Did you sense any changes in temperature? Was the aura equal in size in all directions?

This exercise, once again, strengthens your third-eye and reconnects you with your intuition. Continue to practice with several volunteers of both sexes.

Perceiving Energy

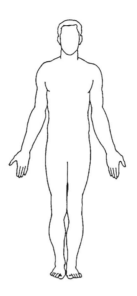

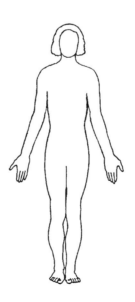

Dawn E. Clark

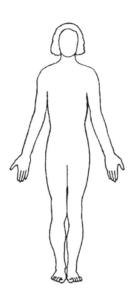

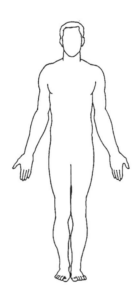

Changing the Field

Again, continuing with a partner from the previous exercise would be advantageous. If you change partners, begin by scanning the size and determining the color of your new partner's aura. Record your findings. Please read the entire exercise before beginning.

1. Position yourself to the side and slightly in front of your partner, so that your left hand can scan the energy in front of the heart chakra.

2. Beginning approximately three feet in front of your partner's heart chakra, gently scan in until you are approximately one to one-half foot from your subject's physical body.

3. At this point stop and sense what you are feeling. Is the energy field dense? Does it feel warm or cold? Does it tingle or prickle your skin?

4. With your hand still in position, close your eyes and silently ask what color you are sensing.

5. Once you have the answer, remain in position with your eyes closed and your hand approximately one to one-half foot in front of your partner's heart chakra. Now, have your partner visualize herself or himself surrounded by a dense, white cloud of universal light and love.

6. Simultaneously, you should visualize your partner being surrounded in white light and unconditional, universal love.

7. Do you feel the difference in your partner's field as you both visualize this positive energy showering down? What color is the energy you are perceiving in your partner's field now?

8. What changes occurred in your partner's aura when you did this? Did the size or the density change? Did you notice a change in the color your third-eye perceived? Did the energy become warmer or softer?

You can expand this exercise by having your partner visualize a negative or hurtful situation. Assess how emotion and projection of positive and negative thoughts affect the aura. Negative emotions tend to substantially contract the aura and/or create a sensation of cold in the energy body.

8
EMPATHY

As you begin tactilely perceiving the Human Energy Field, understanding the energetic mechanics of empathy can be insightful. When someone truly empathizes, what is actually happening is that for a brief moment the empathizer projects a portion of their energy field into another person's emotional layer of aura. This is a type of field interaction.

During that brief touching encounter, the empathizer can experience the other person's pain, joy, anguish, etc. firsthand, as if it were their own.

If you are empathizing with someone who is in distress, for example, it is a good idea to pull your energy back once you have "felt" or experienced their emotions. This allows you to remain stable and better enables you to help them. By not pulling your energy back, you both suffer.

It is also important to understand that those with heightened perception may experience some of this awareness while tactilely scanning the emotional level of the Human Energy Field. So, if this occurs and you begin experiencing emotions which are not your own, don't be alarmed. The sensation will end as soon as you move out of that auric layer. You will, however, be left with a greater appreciation and understanding of that person's emotional state.

9
VISUAL PERCEPTION OF AURA

Visual perception of energy usually takes longer to develop than tactile or intuitive perception. For most people, development of the physical eyes and optic nerves is necessary for them to be able to see the vibrational frequencies associated with color in aura. Some people, however, see auric colors spontaneously as they become increasingly more sensitive to higher vibrating energies. Reawakening your inherent ability to see aura may require time and practice.

Strengthening Optic Perception

To speed your progress, the following exercise will

help you develop your physical eyes to very subtle energies; however, a little preparation is necessary. You will need white index cards, a pencil or pen, a ruler or stencils, and bright, vibrant markers as indicated.

1. On the first card draw a triangle. Use a ruler to be sure you have finite edges. Color the entire triangle, including the edges, bright red.

2. On the second card, draw a crescent moon and color it vibrant orange, positioning it as shown.

3. On the third card, draw a solid yellow square. Be sure to use a ruler.

4. On the fourth card, draw a bright blue circle.

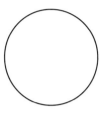

5. On the fifth card, draw a grass green star.

6. On the sixth card, draw a vibrant purple diamond shape as shown.

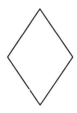

These brightly colored image cards will now be used to help develop your physical eyes for auric perception.

Instructions for use of the cards:

To work with the color image cards you will need to find a blank, light colored wall or ceiling.

1. Use each card one at a time.

2. Hold the card at eye level and at arm's length (approximately 18 to 20 inches from eyes).

3. Stare at the color image on the card without blinking, while counting slowly from 1 to 15.

4. When you reach 15, remove the card quickly from view and immediately direct your gaze to a light colored, blank wall or ceiling.

5. When you look at the wall, you will see the same shape floating in front of you, but this afterimage will appear different in color. Where the original image was green, for example, the afterimage will be red. This lingering image will be soft and translucent in nature, very similar to how auric energies appear to the physical eye.

6. Continue staring at the image until the shape disappears.

7. Repeat with each card.

The technical name for this amazing visual effect is *successive contrast*. Ten to fifteen minutes a day of this exercise is more than enough. The optic nerve is being trained to be more sensitive to higher vibrating energies and dimensions. Over the course of a few weeks, the more you use these cards, the easier these energies will be to perceive.

You may also notice that some of the afterimages associated with the colored shapes are easier to see than others. This is because colors vibrate at varying frequencies and it may take time for your eyes to attune to the entire spectrum.

Now, let's turn our focus to nature and see the aura radiating from trees.

Visual Perception of Tree Auras

Go again to an outdoor area, such as a park, which has many healthy trees. Dusk is the easiest time to begin visually perceiving auric energies if you have never seen them before.

Please read through the entire exercise before beginning. You will need a pencil for sketching.

1. Look around. One tree will seem to draw your attention.

2. Walk over to that tree and thank it silently for helping you learn.

3. Then, step back and stand approximately 15 to 20 feet away from the tree.

4. Focus your attention toward the base of the tree, approximately 6 to 18 inches above the ground and approximately 0 to 6 inches from the side of tree trunk.

5. Direct your gaze *through* this area, looking beyond the tree itself. You are gazing through a very dense energy field.

6. Continue to allow yourself to stare through this energy field, not focusing your vision directly on anything. Most people initially perceive tree auras as wavy lines of energy, almost like the heat waves that waft off the top of a mirage on a hot desert highway. You may also notice that the region behind this energy field appears to be out of focus or distorted. Some perceive tree's energy as whitish in color. Be patient. Keep looking. The energy is there. Record your findings in the following space provided.

7. Practice with several trees, being sure to always thank the trees for participating in your learning experience.

Trees are an excellent place to begin seeing auras because of the density of their energetic fields. As your perception heightens, you will be able to see auras around plants, bushes, flowers, the grass, etc.

PERCEIVING ENERGY

Record your perceptions here:

VISUALLY PERCEIVING THE HUMAN ENERGY FIELD

Your auric bubble extends at least three to six feet in all directions. You must look through it at all times, even when you are trying to perceive someone else's energy field. The following exercise helps you see your own aura, so that over time you will become familiar with your field and be able to discern the difference between your aura and others.

Visually Perceiving Your Own Aura

Observing your own aura can be done while lying in bed and looking up at the ceiling. Dim lighting is most conducive for heightened perception.

1. Warm up briefly with the color image cards.

2. Lie in bed with the lights dimmed.

3. Take a few deep, relaxing breaths.

4. Look towards the ceiling and take your eyes slightly out of focus. In other words, don't focus your eyes sharply on anything.

5. After a few moments you will begin to notice little glimmers or sparkles of light floating around like specks of dust. Be patient. Take your time. These glimmers are part of the energy in your aura. You might even see a haze or flash of color.

PERCEIVING ENERGY

Modification 1:

6. Next, try holding your hands up. Slightly spread your fingers and look at the spaces between them.

7. Slowly bring your fingers back together and then spread them apart again. Do this several times.

8. Can you see any sparkles, colors or energetic densities between the fingers as they open and close? The energy often appears clear at first, like heat waves emanating from a radiator or mirage.

Modification 2:

9. Now try touching both of your hands together at the fingertips and then slowly moving them about five inches apart.

10. Bring them back together again, and then apart again.

11. Can you see any density, sparkles or streams of energy flowing between your fingertips?

12. Next, try imagining your breath flowing down your right arm and out the fingertips of your right hand toward the fingertips of your left hand. How does this change what you see?

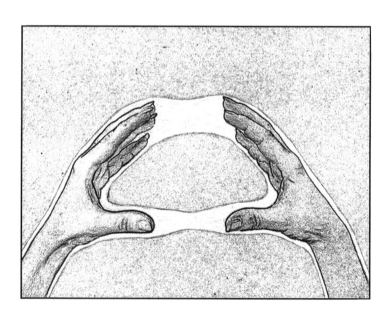

With continued practice your visual perception will rapidly improve.

Visually Perceiving Someone Else's Aura

Seeing aura or energy around others is the next step. The most common initial optical perception is a white or yellowish haze just above the shoulders or around the head. For this exercise you will need a partner.

1. Have your partner stand approximately one to two feet in front of a light colored background or wall.

2. Look through the area just above the person's shoulder, taking your eyes out of focus. In other words, look beyond the person's shoulder area, *though* the energy field, not directly at it. Don't focus your eyes sharply on anything. Most people will initially see a light colored haze or cloud of energy just above the round of the shoulder.

3. Sketch what you perceived on the diagram provided on the next page.

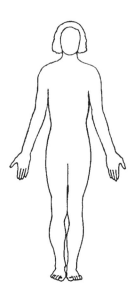

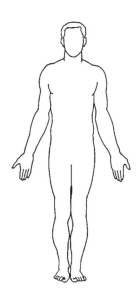

Visual Perception of Color in the Aura

Seeing color in aura generally requires substantial development of the optic nerve and training of the eye itself. However, as you heighten your other sensory perceptions and elevate your own vibrational resonance, seeing color in aura can occur spontaneously. One day you may be looking at someone who is newly in love and suddenly notice a cloud of green floating over their heart chakra. Or, perhaps you will see someone with a black spot in the energy over their lung or breast, only to later learn they have cancer.

Colors in aura can range from solid to translucent in appearance and from pastel to vibrant in hue. Furthermore, the field of color can expand or shrink, and will vary depending on which level of aura you are looking at. Grayed colors are reflective of blocked energy flow or of negative thoughts and emotions.

There are usually at least seven colors appearing in the aura at any one time, with a variety of shades and hues. Much has been written about the meaning of color in aura. The following are brief descriptions of commonly held beliefs regarding the meaning of specific auric colors. I, however, do not believe color should be used as a conclusive means of evaluation. Individuals are unique and present many subtle color variations. Intuitive guidance should be used when interpreting individual findings.

Color Descriptions

Red: densest color; emotions associated range from passion and anger to the soft glow of love and affection. Dark red is usually reflective of stagnant anger. Because of it's density, red is one of the easiest color to perceive. Red-orange is related to sexual passion.

Orange: color of vitality, vigor, ambition, good health and sexual excitement. Dull orange surrounded by burnt orange can reflect burnout or fatigue.

Yellow: color of creativity, intellect and inspiration.

Green: color of health, healing and nurture. Green often radiates from the heart chakra when someone is newly in love.

Blue: indicative of good communication skills, sensitivity and often represents calm, inner-peace and spirituality.

Purple: a highly sensitive color; reflective of a deep connection with spirit, thereby providing a combination of wisdom and understanding; reflective of a true ability to empathize.

Indigo or Deep Purple-Blue: reflects an even deeper connection to spirit.

Earth Colors: are reflective of a connection with grounding earth energies. These colors are often seen when someone is undergoing a growth process and is seeking grounding for nurture and stability during change.

Lavender: this high vibrational energy is often utilized by master teachers to raise the consciousness of others and transmute the vibrations of surrounding energy.

Silver: reflects an awakening of consciousness to the universe and its laws, as well as prosperity consciousness and an opening to a life filled with abundance.

Gold: color of the higher self; can provide great healing and protection from negativity; and is reflective of service to humankind and universal love. Gold is also a master teacher vibration that can transmute energies and raise consciousness.

White: reflects truth; can be used as a protective shield in that it reflects other colors.

Gray: seen in areas with blocked energy flow, emotional shutdown or disease.

Black: seen in areas of total energy blockage, shutdown or disease.

A good indicator of the predominant colors in your auric field is the clothes you choose to wear. Have you ever noticed how on some days certain clothes don't feel right? Have you ever changed your outfit several times before going somewhere? You will feel best when the colors of your clothes compliment the vibrational energies of the colors in your aura that day.

Developing Visual Color Perception of Your Own Aura

Let us begin by expanding on the previous exercise for perceiving one's own aura.

1. Warm up briefly with the color cards.

2. Lie in bed with the lights dimmed.

3. Take a few deep, relaxing breaths.

4. Close your eyes and visualize white light coming in through your crown chakra and forming a ball in the center of your body.

5. Once this ball has formed, open your eyes, hold your right hand up and begin sending energy from the ball through your right arm and out your fingertips, upward towards the ceiling. If you have trouble sending energy, close your eyes for a moment and visualize the energy traveling from the ball in the center of your body, down your arm and out your fingertips. Then open your eyes again for the next step.

6. Spread your fingers apart and then bring them back together. Do this slowly several times.

7. While you are opening and closing your fingers, visualize yourself projecting different colors,

one at a time, through your fingertips. You may just get glimpses of color at first. The colors may appear as sparkles or faint clouds. You may think you see something, only to have it disappear when you focus your attention and look directly at it.

8. Continue to practice with a spectrum of colors. Remember, because of the varying vibrational frequencies of colors, you may be able to see some easier than others.

Adding Sound:

9. Continue sending energy out of your fingertips, and begin humming a tone at different pitches. Perhaps even go up and down a musical scale.

10. See what happens. Go slowly. Take your time. How does the color or density of the energy change in relation to the tone of the humming? Remember some color vibrations are more readily perceptible than others.

Two Hands:

11. A variation of this exercise is to direct energy from one hand to the other through the fingertips.

With continued practice seeing your own auric colors becomes ever easier.

Seeing Color in Aura I

This exercise in perceiving auric color allows your mind's-eye to supplement what your physical eyes are seeing. You will need a partner and crayons. Please use the following diagrams and read the entire exercise before beginning.

1. Warm up briefly with the color image cards.

2. Then, have your partner stand two feet in front of a light colored wall.

3. Look at your partner without blinking for approximately thirty seconds, then close your eyes and allow your third-eye to visualize his/her auric field. Remember, you can perceive your partner's aura even if you can't optically see the colors at this time. Subconsciously you are able to discern differing color vibrations and energy fields. Allow your intuition to guide you.

4. Open your eyes and immediately color what you saw in your visualization on the following diagram.

5. When you are finished coloring, close your eyes again and see if more information appears, but do not look back up at your partner.

PERCEIVING ENERGY

6. Repeat the process of sketching and visualizing what your mind's-eye presents until you feel you are finished.

This exercise allows your mind's-eye to paint the picture of what your physical eyes are beginning to see and to correlate it with what you are intuitively sensing. It is a good idea to repeat this exercise with several volunteers of both sexes. What differences do you notice?

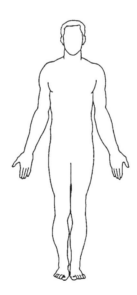

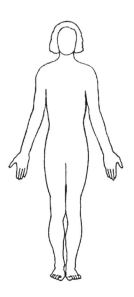

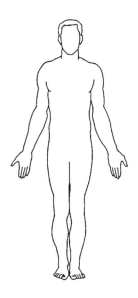

Seeing Color in Aura II

In this exercise you will be catching a visual image of your partner's energy in a glimpse or "snap shot." This quick glimpse trains your physical eye, while simultaneously utilizing your other senses as well. You will need a partner and a box of crayons. Please use the diagrams provided and read the entire exercise before beginning.

1. Warm up briefly with the color image cards.

2. Have your partner stand two feet in front of a light colored wall.

3. Look at your partner's entire form and the immediate surrounding area without blinking for ten seconds. Do not focus on anything in particular; simply try to take in the visual image in its entirety.

4. Then, immediately direct your attention to your diagram. Quickly choose colors of crayons that attract your attention and draw them where you *think* they should go. You may feel like you're making up what you see. Trust your intuition. Perception occurs on many different levels.

5. Complete your coloring as fast as possible.

Allow your intuition to guide you. Apply color wherever it feels appropriate. Sometimes you may want to press hard and sometimes soft to show the intensity of the energy. You may feel the desire to make swirls, squiggles, straight lines or clouds to show the energy.

6. As you apply one color, the area for that color may expand to multiple locations. All the while, a new color may be emerging into your awareness.

7. Never second-guess the color that your hand is directing you to. It is usually the correct one. Remember, it is the ego that causes us to doubt our first intuitive impressions. If the shade you initially chose doesn't feel right, exchange it for another. Don't look back up at your partner until you are completely finished. This portion of the exercise should take no more than a minute or two.

8. When you have finished coloring your diagram, look at your partner again and envision the same color scheme that you drew. This portion of the exercise develops your physical sight in conjunction with what you have already intuitively perceived.

Based on my experience, with just a little practice most people can see one to three colors with 60-80% accuracy. It's highly beneficial to repeat this exercise with several volunteers of both sexes before proceeding with the next exercise.

Perceiving Energy

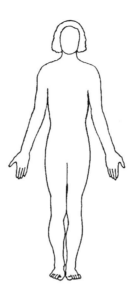

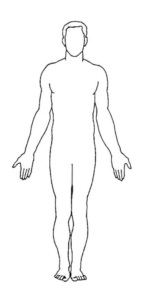

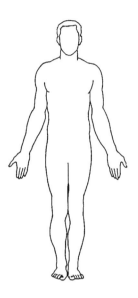

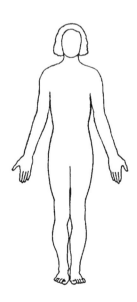

Seeing Color in Aura III

Let us continue developing your perceptual abilities by going beyond the "snap shot" approach to seeing aura. You will need a partner and a box of crayons. Please use the following diagrams and read the entire exercise before beginning.

1. Warm up briefly with the color image cards.

2. Have your partner stand two feet in front of a light colored wall.

3. Look at your partner's entire form and the immediate surrounding area for 45-60 seconds.

4. Then, move immediately to the diagram and color your perceptions. You may not know what to color until you shift your focus to the diagram. At that point you will be guided which color to choose and where to place it.

    Don't spend too long looking at the aura before you begin to color or you may miss an image. Often people want to see too much at once, and when they finally begin to color they can't remember all that they have seen.

5. Allow your intuition to guide you. Complete your coloring as fast as possible. Apply color

wherever it feels appropriate. Press hard or soft to show the intensity of the energy. Make squiggles, waves, swirls or clouds to show the energetic flow. Allow your inner guidance freedom to direct you without judgement.

6. As you apply one color, the area for that color may expand to multiple locations, while a new color is emerging into your consciousness.

7. Normally you will get two or three different impressions associated with the first. Never second-guess the color that your hand is directing you to, because it is usually the correct one. If the shade you initially chose doesn't feel right, exchange it for another. Don't look at your partner again until you feel you are completely finished recording the information you have perceived.

8. When you have finished coloring your initial perceptions, continue the exercise by looking at your partner again for 45-60 seconds more.

9. Color the diagram with your new impressions. To avoid fatiguing your eyes and confusing your perceptions, the entire exercise should last no more than 3-5 minutes.

At this point, you may begin perceiving black or grayed areas in the aura, in addition to colors. These areas often reflect energetic blockages or slowed areas of energy flow. Color these on your diagrams as well.

Practice with volunteers of both sexes to increase your proficiency.

Perceiving Energy

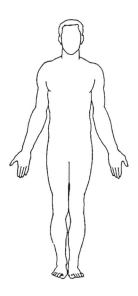

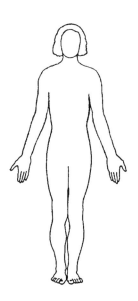

Dawn E. Clark

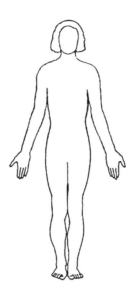

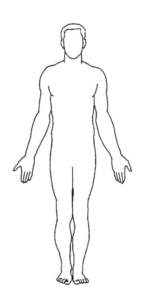

Auric Time Zones

As your visual and intuitive abilities to see and interpret auric information increase, you may begin to perceive that a person's auric field reflects a progression of events, as well as energies a person has projected for future manifestation.

The following diagram reflects this energetic auric progression. It is important to understand, however, that these zones are flexible.

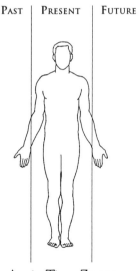

Auric Time Zones

The directional flow of these auric time zones tends to differ depending on whether a person lives north or south of the equator. It is a commonly held belief that energy circulates from left to right above the equator, as is often seen by the direction water flows as it swirls down a drain. South of the equator, energy circulates from right to left.

So, for those of us living in the Northern Hemisphere, incoming or future energy lies in the left side of the auric field and reflects energy projections made for future manifestation. Information about the present is generally located above and closely surrounding the body, and the right side of our aura tends to contain information about events that have already occurred.

Did you ever wonder how psychics foretell your future? It's easy. They read the energy projections you have made through thought, belief and verbalization in the future side of your aura. For example, if you spend time visualizing yourself having a new car, a new job, or a new lover, and you constantly talk about it as well, these energy projections would be present and perceivable in the left side of your aura.

Likewise, if you hold negative beliefs or make negative statements, such as "I'll never find that special someone to share my life with," or "I'll never have enough money," chances are you won't, and those projections would also be perceivable. Thoughts and words have energy. You manifest that which you say and believe through your energetic projections.

Many people, without realizing their own creative abilities, believe carte blanche that what a psychic says will come true. After a psychic reading, they proceed to invest more time and energy talking and thinking about the psychic's predictions. In doing so, they create a self-fulfilling prophecy.

Others go to psychics and scoff at what they foretell. But, by later talking about the predictions with friends, or thinking about them, energy is invested in the predictions, thereby contributing to their manifestation.

Be aware of where and how you invest your energy. I am not suggesting never to have a psychic reading done, I am merely encouraging you to take it at face value. If you hear something you don't like – change it. You have the power to change future energy projections merely by changing thought patterns, beliefs and verbalizations. You have the power to manifest the life you desire.

10
AUDITORY CLAIRVOYANCE

Colors vibrate at a particular sound and so do people. The energetic signature of an individual has a unique resonance. At first you may perceive this resonance intuitively with a sense of knowing. As you develop your auditory clairvoyant abilities, however, you may actually begin hearing audible sounds.

The sounds emanating from energetic vibrations can be perceived and compared by pitch and frequency. Pitch refers to the highness or lowness of a sound, and frequency refers to the number of complete cycles per second of a sound wave. Just like in music, notes with a low pitch will have a slower rate of vibration or frequency than those with a high pitch.

Pitch and frequency vary depending on a number of factors, such as the amount of energetic blockages a person has, energy flow through chakra centers, state of enlightenment, soul density and overall mental, physical and spiritual well-being.

Hearing Energetic Vibrations I

For this exercise you will need several participants, one volunteer and a group facilitator. Please read the entire exercise before beginning.

1. Have one volunteer leave the room and wait outside with the facilitator.

2. Have all other participants form a half-circle, sit quietly with hands turned palm upward, and face the door where the volunteer will enter.

3. Then, have the participants close their eyes and quiet their minds.

4. Participants should listen to how the room sounds and make a mental note of their perceptions.

5. After this, the facilitator should quietly direct the volunteer to enter the room and notify the group of the volunteer's entrance.

6. At this point, the participants should attempt to "hear" a perceptible difference between how the room sounded before and after the volunteer entered. The difference may be very subtle.

PERCEIVING ENERGY

7. If an audible difference can't be "heard", they should rely on their intuitive clairvoyance to perceive the difference in sound vibration. Did the pitch go up or down? Was the frequency faster or slower in the room after the volunteer entered?

8. Record your answers in the space below following the model as shown. Compare answers.

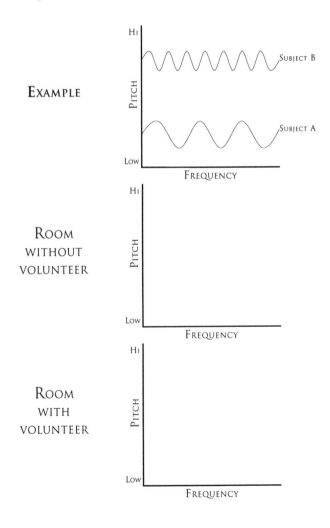

Hearing Energetic Vibrations II

Let us expand the exercise. This time you will need several participants, two volunteers and a group facilitator. Please read the entire exercise before beginning.

1. Have two volunteers leave the room and wait outside with the facilitator.

2. All other participants should form a half-circle, sit quietly with hands turned palm upward, and face the door where the volunteers will enter.

3. Have all participants close their eyes and quiet their minds.

4. Participants should take a moment to hear how the room sounds and make a mental note of their perceptions.

5. Once all participants have done this, the facilitator should quietly direct one volunteer to enter the room. He should then notify the participants of the volunteer's entrance.

6. The participants should tune in and listen for an audible difference between how the room sounded before and after the volunteer entered the room. The difference may be very subtle.

PERCEIVING ENERGY

7. If an audible difference can't be "heard," they should rely on their intuitive clairvoyance to perceive the difference in sound vibration.

8. Did the pitch go up or down? Was the frequency faster or slower in the room after the volunteer entered?

9. After a moment the facilitator should quietly send in the other volunteer to stand next to the first and notify the group of the second volunteer's entrance.

10. Once again, the group should listen for an "audible" difference or an intuitive knowing of how the sound vibration changed when the second volunteer entered the room.

11. Record your answers in the space below and on the following page. Compare answers.

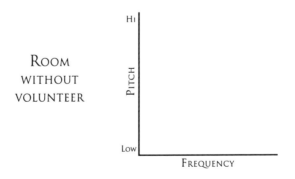

ROOM WITHOUT VOLUNTEER

105

Room with one volunteer

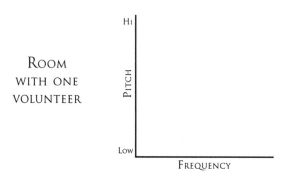

Room with two volunteers

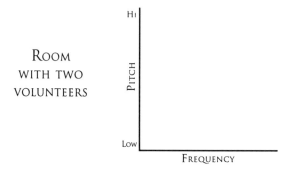

Hearing Energetic Vibrations III

For this exercise your will need several participants, a male and female volunteer and a facilitator. Please read the entire exercise before beginning.

1. Have a male and a female volunteer leave the room. The volunteers should take off their shoes, so that when they re-enter the room the group won't be able to distinguish their footsteps. The volunteers should then wait outside with the facilitator until the group is ready.

2. Have all other participants form a half-circle, sit quietly with hands turned palm upward, and face the door where the volunteers will enter.

3. At this point, have all participants close their eyes, quiet their minds and perceive the sound of the room.

4. Once all participants have done this, the facilitator should quietly direct one of the volunteers to enter the room and announce the arrival of the volunteer to the group, being careful not to identify the volunteer's sex.

5. Keeping their eyes closed, the group of participants should listen for an audible difference after the volunteer has entered the room.

6. After approximately 30-45 seconds, the facilitator should quietly motion the volunteer to leave and tell the participants that the volunteer has left.

7. The participants should then open their eyes and record their findings on the following two diagrams.

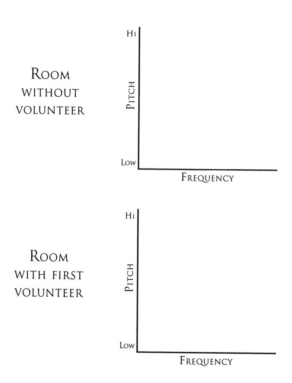

8. Once finished recording, the participants should again close their eyes. After a few seconds, the facilitator should quietly motion for the volunteer of the opposite sex to enter the room. The facilitator should then notify the group that the next volunteer has entered, once

again being careful not to identify the volunteer's sex.

9. The group of participants should then listen for the sound vibrations of the second volunteer. Is the pitch higher or lower? Is the frequency faster or slower?

10. If they aren't able to audibly "hear" a difference, how does their intuition perceive the sound vibration?

11. After a moment, the facilitator should quietly motion for the volunteer to leave and notify the group when the volunteer is out of sight.

12. Participants should then open their eyes and record their findings on the following diagram.

13. Compare your answers and have the volunteers come forward. How did the findings relate to the sexes of the volunteers? What differences were perceived between the volunteer's pitches and frequencies?

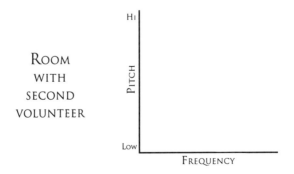

ROOM WITH SECOND VOLUNTEER

Your auditory clairvoyance will continue to increase over time with practice. You may even find that one ear has greater sensory perception than the other. As you become more aware of new dimensions, you may also notice an occasional high pitched buzzing in your ear or an apparent temporary loss of hearing from time to time. These occurrences are often indicative of "tuning in" to information carried at a higher frequency than what you are accustomed to hearing. The new information you receive from this "tuning in" will unfold in your conscious mind as insights, guidance or higher understanding.

11
PSYCHOMETRY

Psychometry is the perception of facts concerning an object or its owner through contact with the object's energy field. Objects closely held by people, such as rings, watches, jewelry, wallets or purses, retain traces of their owner's energetic vibrations. Through these lingering energies, the emotions and thoughts of that person can be readily perceived by anyone who chooses to develop their intuitive perceptual abilities.

Practicing Psychometry
For this exercise have a friend bring you an ob-

ject belonging to someone else. Be sure this is a closely held object. Also, please note that plastics and other man-made fabrics do not retain vibrations. Items composed of natural materials such as metals, wood, leather, stones, or gems are good for psychometry. Try using keys, jewelry, watches, rings, wallets, or purses. A cotton blanket that is used every night will also work.

1. Quite yourself and close your eyes while holding the object loosely in your hands.

2. Shift the object back and forth between your hands.

3. Focus your attention on the object's energy.

4. After a moment or two you will begin to get impressions about the owner. Some of these perceptions may come in the form of intuitive knowings, while others may be visualizations. You may even perceive affiliated odors with your heightened sense of smell.

5. Begin talking about what you're perceiving as soon as possible. Verbalizing what you are sensing will assist the flow of information. You should verbalize even your slightest impressions.

Generally speaking, after practicing a few times, most students in my classes are able to perceive answers to basic questions with over 60% accuracy. Take time to pat yourself on the back and validate your perceptual abilities every time you read an object's energy correctly. Positive reinforcement and acknowledgement go a long way toward self-confidence and further encourage your sensory abilities.

If psychometry is something you wish to become proficient at, keep practicing all forms of heightened perception and your skill will grow.

12
THE ENERGY OF PLACES

In addition to having their own natural energy, places or localities also hold the energetic vibrations of the people who have lived there. Strong emotions emitted during events that transpired leave heavy energetic residue behind.

When visiting places where intense emotions occurred, such as concentration camps, battlefields or dungeons, those who are perceptually sensitive often experience clairvoyant flashbacks to the events that transpired. These flashbacks may take the form of inner knowings, visual images, smells, sounds, tastes, or other physical sensations.

You, too, can add new dimensions to sightseeing by continuing to heighten your perceptual abilities.

13
PERCEIVING GUIDES

Have you ever sensed someone standing behind you? But, when you turned to look there was no one there. Did you ever think you caught a glimpse of someone out of the corner of your eye? But, when you looked the room was empty. These sensings are how most people perceive angels or guides.

Actually seeing or tangibly sensing these energetic beings requires heightened perceptual abilities. These spirits vibrate at such a high frequency that they are practically invisible or imperceptible to most.

How to Perceive Angels or Guides

When you actively seek to perceive angels or

guides, they often will slow their vibration down momentarily for you to perceive them. The following are guidelines for perceiving these energetic beings.

1. At first you can usually feel or vaguely sense a presence in the area. Your intuition will tell you that you have "company," and your ego will often argue saying, "That's silly."

2. Once you become aware of the presence of a spirit guide, quiet your mind so you can tune in to the perception.

3. Close your eyes and allow your mind's-eye to form an image of where the angel or guide is, and how it appears.

4. At this point you can try communicating with the angel or guide by telepathically projecting your thoughts and allowing yourself to visualize the interaction, or by choosing to open your eyes and trying to actually see it.

5. If you choose to see it with your physical eyes, direct your attention to where your mind's-eye sensed the guide was. Then quiet your mind and relax.

6. The image usually begins to materialize as a differing energetic density, a transparent cloud of white or colored energy, gold sparkles, or as a faint outline. Guides and angels appear in many different forms. Often they materialize in a form that they believe will bring you comfort or provide you information.

7. You may see the spirit's appearance only for a second. This flash of an image may be so quick that your physical eye barely perceived it.

8. Close your eyes again and allow your mind's-eye to fill in the gaps. Try to remember what you see in your visualization as it is revealed to you.

9. Guides or angels usually have something to share with you. In order to hear their messages, you must clear your mind. Most people perceive these messages as quiet knowings. Those with auditory clairvoyance may actually hear words or sounds that are distinct and clear. Accept that which is presented to you along with any associated pictures and intuitive knowings.

10. Sketch and/or journal your impressions as quickly as possible. The meaning of what was presented to you usually becomes clear over time.

Along with the visual, intuitive and sensory perception of spirit guides, another common way to experience their presence is through smell or olfactory clairvoyance. You may be walking through a room, when all of a sudden you are overcome with the rich aroma of vanilla, an intense floral scent, or some other distinct smell where none should be. These scents tend to linger in clouds and smell purer than they do in their everyday versions.

When you encounter these aromas, close your

eyes and ask what you are to learn or gain from the experience. The answer will usually pop into your head.

14
SENSE THE DIFFERENCE

With heightened sensory perceptions you will be ever more aware of the energetic dynamics which surround you. Your abilities to perceive energy fields can be translated to many areas of your life.

In relationships, you will be more aware of other's true feelings and have a deeper understanding of the interactions that take place, thereby fostering more meaningful relationships. Enhanced sensory perception also heightens intimacy and adds new dimension to physical pleasures. The energetic body orgasm is a reality.

Another benefit of increased perceptual abilities is the ability to sense when someone's spoken words don't match their energetic projections. Hidden agendas will no longer be hidden.

More importantly, by understanding how thoughts affect energy fields and in turn health, we are empowered to create a happy, healthy, prosperous life. Let imagination and intuition guide you as you apply what you've learned.

The process of developing your sensory awareness beyond normal perceptual ranges is a natural evolutionary step. You have the ability to be clairvoyant and to fully experience the world around you. All that is required is practice, and you, too, can perceive energy beyond the physical form.

RESOURCES

Being able to readily access your intuition greatly facilitates heightened sensory perception. Additionally, the perception of energy is fostered by elevating your own vibration level through an opening of energy centers, recovering lost energetic density and healing core life issues.

We highly recommend *Gifts for the Soul* and *Tuning In (audio cassette)* for those wishing to expand their abilities.

These books and other titles by Dawn E. Clark, Ph.D. are available through your local bookstore, or you can:

Order on line at:
www.infinite-energylinks.com

For your convenience, the following order form may be copied or cut out for fax or mail orders. For fax orders, please include your credit card information.

Order by Fax, or Phone Aarron Productions
Fax:(281) 359-1069
Phone:(281) 359-5154

Order by Mail: For mail orders, please enclose check, money order or credit card information.

Infinite EnergyLinks, Inc.
P.O. Box 5485
Kingwood, TX 77325-5485

Order Form

Name _____

Address _____
                               Street

          _____
             City   State   Zip

TITLE	QTY.	TOTAL
Gifts for the Soul: A Guided Journey of Discovery, Transformation and Infinite Possibilities (Hardcover) $ 23.00		
Perceiving Energy: Beyond the Physical Form (Paperback) 12.95		
Tuning In: Opening Your Intuitive Channels (Audiobook: approx running time 3 hours) 15.95		
Less 10% discount for multiple orders		
(TX Residents Only) 8.25% Sales Tax		
Shipping and Handling (see below)		
Total		

Shipping and Handling: 1 book @ 3.95, each additional book add $1.75
All orders shipped within 48 hours of receipt.

For credit card orders: We accept Visa, MasterCard, and American Express.

Credit Card Number

                          _____
Signature

                          _____
Exp.

                          _____

Now Find Dawn Clark on the Web at:

www.dawnclark.net